Latin Quips at Your Fingertips

Latin Quips at Your Fingertips

Witty Latin Sayings by Wise Romans

Compiled and
translated by
ROSE WILLIAMS

FALL RIVER PRESS

Originally published in the United Kingdom as *Going to Hades Is Easy*

This 2001 edition published by Fall River Press,
by arrangement with Michael O'Mara Books Limited.

Fall River Press
122 Fifth Avenue
New York, NY 10011

ISBN-13: 978-0-7607-2538-2
ISBN-10: 0-7607-2538-1

Printed and bound in the United States of America

11   13   15   17   19   20   18   16   14   12   10

❖ CONTENTS ❖

This little book has two good points:
it has good laughs and it makes good sense.

Duplex libelli dos est: quod risum movet
et quod prudenti vitam consilio movet.

Phaedrus, *Fabulae* I, Prologus 3

❖ WISE WORDS ❖

Fear, not kindness, restrains the wicked.

Metus improbos compescit, non clementia.

Syrus, *Maxims*

Laugh at life; don't cry over it.

Humanius est deridere vitam quam deplorare.

Seneca the Younger, *De Tranquillitate Animi*, III, 8

Don't whistle and drink at the same time.

Noli simul flare sorbereque.

Plautus, *Mostellaria*, 79

You pray for good health and a body that will be strong in old age. Good – but your rich foods block the gods' answer and tie Jupiter's hands.

Poscis opem nervis corpusque fidele senectae. Esto, age – sed grandes patinae tuccetaque crassa adnuere his superos vetuere Iovemque morantur.

Persius, *Saturae*, II, 41-43

**When healthy, we all have wonderful
advice for the sick.**

Facile omnes quom valemus recta consilia
aegrotis damus.

Terence, *Andria*, 67

**I've seen many men avoid the region of good
advice before they were really near it.**

Ego multos saepe vidi regionem fugere consili prius
quam repertam haberent.

Plautus, *Miles Gloriosus*, 885

**Few people can distinguish between true good
things and their opposites; in city or war camp,
we seek what will be our ruin.**

Pauci dinoscere possunt vera bona atque illis multum
diversa; nocitura toga, nocitura petuntur militia.

Juvenal, *Satirae*, X, 3, 8

**What you didn't hope for happens more
often than what you hoped for.**

Insperata accidunt magis saepe quam quae speres.

Plautus, *Mostellaria*, 197

Old Cato always wondered how two fortune-tellers could look at each other without laughing.

Vetus illud Catonis admodum scitum est, qui mirari se aiebat quod non rideret haruspex haruspicem cum vidisset.

Cicero, *De Divinatione*, II, 51

It's too late to ask advice when the danger comes.

Sero in periculis est consilium quaerere.

Syrus, *Maxims*

When you have just climbed out of a deep well and are perched on top, you are in the greatest danger of falling in again.

Non tu scis, quom et alto puteo sursum ad summum escenderis, maximum periclum inde esse ab summo ne rursum cadas.

Plautus, *Miles Gloriosus*, 1150-1151

Nobody underestimates his own troubles.

Neque cuiquam mortalium iniuriae suae parvae videntur.

Sallust, *Bellum Catilinae*, Caesar's Speech

**A man needs a good mirror to scrutinize
his heart as well as his face.**

Non oris causa modo homines aequom fuit sibi habere
speculum, sed qui perspicere possent cor sapientiae.

Plautus, *Epidicus*, 382-383

**It's stupid to complain about misfortune
that is your own fault.**

Stultum est queri de adversis, ubi culpa est tua.

Syrus, *Maxims*

**Though your threshers provide a hundred
thousand bushels of grain, your stomach still can hold
no more than mine.**

Milia frumenti tua triverit area centum, non tuus hoc
capiet venter plus ac meus.

Horace, *Satirae*, I, 1, 46-47

**It's better to profit by a horrible example
than to be one.**

Te de aliis, quam alios de te suaviust fieri doctos.

Plautus, *Persa*, 540

Life is short, but troubles make it longer.

Brevis ipsa vita est sed malis fit longior.

Syrus, *Maxims*

The man you want to keep bound to you should be chained by food and drink.

Quem tu adservare recte, ne aufugiat, voles, esca atque potione vinciri decet.

Plautus, *Menaechmi*, 87-88

If fortune wants to do you in, she makes you stupid.

Stultum facit fortuna quem vult perdere.

Syrus, *Maxims*

Everybody lives; not everybody deserves to.

Vivere commune est, sed non commune mereri.

Prudentius, *Contra Orationem Symmachi*, II, 807

The man who inspects the saddle blanket instead of the horse is stupid; most stupid is the man who judges another man by his clothes or his circumstances.

Stultus est qui stratum, non equum
inspicit; stultissimus qui hominem
aut veste aut condicione aestimat.

Seneca the Younger, *Epistulae Morales*, XVII, 23-25

Fortune is glass; just when it gleams brightest it shatters.

Fortuna vitrea est; tum cum splendet frangitur.

Syrus, *Maxims*

When fools try to avoid a vice, they sometimes rush into its opposite.

Dum vitant stulti vitia, in contraria currunt.

Horace, *Satirae*, I, 2, 24

There's no point in seeking a remedy for a thunderbolt.

Remedium frustra est contra fulmen quaerere.

Syrus, *Maxims*

**A fellow who gets more than he deserves wants
more than he gets.**

Cui plus licet quam par est plus vult quam licet.

Syrus (quoted in Macrobius, *Saturnalia*, II, 7)

Nothing moves faster than gossip.

Fama malum quo non aliud velocius ullum.

Virgil, *Aeneid*, IV, 174

A man must have some wit to know he is a fool.

Non pote non sapere qui se stultum intellegit.

Syrus, *Maxims*

**The great thing is to know when to speak and
when to keep quiet.**

Magna res est vocis et silentii temperamentum.

Seneca the Younger (attributed), *Proverbs*, 74

**If we would only become when well, the men we
promised to become when we were sick.**

Utinam tales esse sani perseveremus quales
nos futuros profitemur infirmi.

Pliny the Younger, *Epistulae*, VII, 26

A handsome face is a silent testimonial.

Formosa facies muta commendatio est.

Syrus, *Maxims*

**A fire can't throw a great light without
burning something.**

Late ignis lucere, ut nihil urat, non potest.

Syrus, *Maxims*

**He preferred being a good man to
looking like one.**

Esse quam videri bonus malebat.

Sallust, *Bellum Catilinae*, LIV

No man loses honour who had any in the first place.

Fidem nemo umquam perdit nisi qui non habet.

Syrus, *Maxims*

Speech is given to many; intelligence to few.

Sermo datur cunctis; animi sapientia paucis.

Disticha Moralia

The silence of a stupid man looks like wisdom.

Taciturnitas stulto homini pro sapientia est.

Syrus, *Maxims*

Thrift is misery with a good press agent.

Frugalitas miseria est rumoris boni.

Syrus, *Maxims*

Whatever you want to teach, be brief.

Quidquid praecipies, esto brevis.

Horace, *Ars Poetica*, 333

Good sense, not age, brings wisdom.

Sensus, non aetas, invenit sapientem.

Syrus, *Maxims*

Exuberance is easily corrected; dullness is incurable.

Facile remedium est ubertati; sterilia nullo labore
vincuntur.

Quintilian, *Institutio Oratoria*, II, 4, 6

The bigger the undertaking, the trickier it is.

Res quanto est maior tanto est insidiosior.

Syrus, *Maxims*

Honesty is praised while it starves.

Probitas laudatur et alget.

Juvenal, *Satirae*, I, 74

**It's very important whether a man is wise,
or only looks it.**

Vultu an natura sapiens sis, multum interest.

Syrus, *Maxims*

He who is everywhere is nowhere.

Nusquam est qui ubique est.

Seneca the Younger, *Epistulae Morales*, II, 2

It's dangerous to guard something everybody wants.

Maximo periculo custoditur quod multis placet.

Syrus, *Maxims*

**A traveller with empty pockets can
whistle in a robber's face.**

Cantabit vacuus coram latrone viator.

Juvenal, *Satirae*, X, 22

**It's best to do favours for people with
good memories.**

Optime positum est beneficium ubi meminit qui accipit.

Syrus, *Maxims*

Who will watch the watchmen?

Quis custodiet ipsos custodes?

Juvenal, *Satirae*, VI, 347

It's easier to do a wrong than to endure one.

Iniuriam facilius facias quam feras.

Syrus, *Maxims*

Easy tears show treachery, not grief.

Paratae lacrimae insidias, non fletum, indicant.

Syrus, *Maxims*

God rewards virtue; he shouldn't have to furnish it.

Di immortales virtutem approbare, non adhibere debent.

Gellius (quotation from a speech by
Quintus Metellus Numidicus)

Anger is the one thing made better by delay.

Rei nulli prodest mora nisi iracundiae.

Syrus, *Maxims*

Be careful about starting something you may regret.

Cave quicquam incipias quod paeniteat postea.

Syrus, *Maxims*

**The time will come when looking in
the mirror grieves you, and that grief
will be another cause of wrinkles.**

Tempus erit, quo vos speculum vidisse pigebit,
et veniet rugis altera causa dolor.

Ovid, *De Medicamine Faciei Liber*, 47-48

You ought to watch whatever you can lose.

Adspicere oportet quicquid possis perdere.

Syrus, *Maxims*

Beauty and wisdom don't mix.

Raram fecit mixturam cum sapientia forma.

Petronius, *Satyricon*, 94

**Quod tacitum velis esse, nemini dixeris.
Si tibi ipsi non imperasti, quomodo ab
aliis silentium speras?**

What you want to keep secret, tell no one.
If you could not control your urge to tell, how can you
expect silence from anyone else?

Seneca (attributed), *Proverbs*, 16

It's better to trust in courage than luck.

Virtuti melius fortunae creditur.

Syrus, *Maxims*

Death's unavoidable; let's have a drink.

Bibamus, moriendum est.

Seneca the Elder, *Controversiae*, II, 6, 3

❖ FOLLIES & VICES ❖

Any man can make a mistake; only a fool keeps making the same one.

Cuiusvis hominis est errare; nullius nisi insipientis in errore perseverare.

Cicero, *Philippicae*, XII, 2, 5

You're a rabbit yourself, and you want to hunt!

Lepus tute es, et pulpamentum quaeris!

Livius Andronicus, *Ex Incertis Fabulis*

Make lots of promises: anybody can be rich in them.

Promittas facito: pollicitis dives quilibet esse potest.

Ovid, *Ars Amatoria*, I, 443

**When my neighbour says I'm a wonderful person,
shall I not believe it?**

Egregium cum me vicinia dicat, non credam?

Persius, *Saturae*, IV, 45

Why shouldn't a fellow laugh while he tells the truth?

Quam ridentem dicere verum quid vetat?

Horace, *Satirae*, I, 1, 24

Evil natures never lack teachers.

Malae naturae numquam doctore indigent.

Syrus, *Maxims*

**Even those who don't want to kill anybody
would like the power to do it.**

Et qui nolunt occidere quemquam posse volunt.

Juvenal, *Satirae*, X, 96

His only fault was having none.

Nihil peccat nisi quod nihil peccat.

Pliny the Younger, *Epistulae*, IX, 26

Tears for somebody else's troubles dry quickly.

Cito enim arescit lacrima, praesertim in alienis malis.

Cicero, *De Partitione Oratoria*, 57

**You would have no divinity, Chance, if
we had any sense: we make you a god and
place you in the skies.**

Nullum numen habes, si sit prudentia:
nos te nos facimus, Fortuna, deam
caeloque locamus.

Juvenal, *Satirae*, X, 365-366

Going to Hell is easy; it's coming back that's hard!

Facilis descensus Averno; sed ad auras evadere est labor!

Virgil, *Aeneid*, VI, 126

**What hurt him most was his outrageous opinion
of his own worth.**

Huic maxime putamus malo fuisse nimiam opinionem
ingenii atque virtutis.

Nepos, *Alcibiades*, 7

**Among us, the god most revered is Wealth,
but so far it has no temple of its own.**

Quandoquidem inter nos sanctissima divitiarum
maiestas, esti funesta pecunia templo nondum habitas.

Juvenal, *Satirae*, I, 112-113

Those who can sin in secret do so more quickly.

Omnes qui occulte peccant, peccant ocius.

Syrus, *Maxims*

A man's word of honour is worth as much as the cash he has in his strongbox.

Quantum quisque sua nummorum servat in arca, tantum habet et fidei.

Juvenal, *Satirae*, III, 143-144

We turn virtues upside down and want to soil a clean vessel.
If any honest man lives among us, we call him slow and stupid.

Nos virtutes ipsas invertimus atque sincerum cupimus vas incrustare.
Probus quis nobiscum vivit: illi tardo cognomen, pingui, damus.

Horace, *Satirae*, I, 3, 55-57

Am I to stand idle and unnoticed, so handsome and so heroic, all for nothing?

Hic astabo tantisper cum hac forma et factis frustra?

Plautus, *Miles Gloriosus*, 1021

Pretty boy, complexion isn't everything!

O formose puer, nimium ne crede colori!

Virgil, *Eclogae*, II, 17

Since you can't copy our pleasures, you begrudge them.

Quoniam aemulari non licet, nunc invides.

Plautus, *Miles Gloriosus*, 839

Men easily believe what they want to.

Homines libenter id quod volunt credunt.

Caesar, *De Bello Gallico*, III, 18

I've seen hammers with the handles off cleverer than he is!

Malleum sapientiorem vidi excusso manubrio!

Plautus, *Epidicus*, 525

In Rome you want the country; in the country you brag about town.

Romae rus optas; absentem rusticus urbem tollis ad astras levis.

Horace, *Satirae*, VI, 28

A few are unwilling to sin; everybody knows how.

Peccare pauci nolunt; nulli nesciunt.

Syrus, *Maxims*

They boasted that they had no faults; they also had no virtues.

Satis putant vitio carere; etiam virtutibus carent.

Quintilian, *Institutio Oratoria*, II, 4, 9

**What shall I do in the city?
I don't know how to lie.**

Quid Romae faciam? Mentiri nescio.

Juvenal, *Satirae*, III, 41

It's stupid to stop in the middle of a crime.

Res est profecto stulta nequitiae modus.

Seneca the Younger, *Agamemnon*, 101

A liar better have a good memory.

Mendacem memorem esse oportere.

Quintilian, *Institutio Oratoria*, IV, 2, 91

Lust wants whatever it can't have.

Nil magis amat cupiditas, quam quod non licet.

Syrus, *Maxims*

All singers have this flaw: if asked by friends they will not sing; if unasked, they will not stop.

Omnibus hoc vitium est cantoribus: inter amicos ut numquam inducant animum cantare rogati, iniussi numquam desistant.

Horace, *Satirae*, II, 1-3

A fellow who argues with a drunk is abusing an absent man.

Absentem laedit, cum ebrio qui litigat.

Syrus, *Maxims*

**When a bad man pretends to be good,
he's at his worst.**

Malus bonum ubi se simulat, tunc est pessimus.

Syrus, *Maxims*

**Anything we haven't seen before
is marvellous.**

Omne ignotum pro magnifico est.

Tacitus, *De Vita et Moribus Iulii Agricolae*, 30

**The sick man does himself no favour
when he makes the doctor his heir.**

Male secum agit aeger, medicum qui heredem facit.

Syrus, *Maxims*

Idiot of idiots, to trust what is written!

Stultior stulto fuisti, qui tabellis crederes.

Plautus, *Curculio*, 551

Always depend on people to think the worst.

Nos in vitium credula turba sumus.

Ovid, *Fasti*, IV, 311

No luck is so good that you can't find some complaint.

Nulla tam bona est fortuna de qua nihil possis queri.

Syrus, *Maxims*

Make me chaste and pure, but not yet.

Da mihi castitatem et continentiam, sed noli modo.

St Augustine, *Confessiones*, VIII, 7

A fellow who won't do a favour has no right to ask for one.

Beneficium dare qui nescit iniuste petit.

Syrus, *Maxims*

**I see and praise better things;
I do worse ones.**

Video meliora proboque; deteriora sequor.

Ovid, *Metamorphoses*, VII, 20

**When he says he did you a favour,
he's asking for one.**

Beneficium qui dedisse se dicit petit.

Syrus, *Maxims*

**'I want to be a good man from this day on' – a wish
that won't come true and never has!**

'Bonus volo iam ex hoc die esse' – quod neque fiet
neque fuit.

Plautus, *Persa*, 479

**The difference between bad speech and bad
deeds is opportunity.**

Maledictus a malefico non distat nisi occasione.

Quintilian, *Institutio Oratoria*, XII, 9, 9

MONEY, POLITICS & JUSTICE

Nothing is so well fortified that money cannot capture it.

Nihil tam munitum quod non expugnari pecunia possit

Cicero, *In Verrem*, I, ii, 4

Money should be mastered, not served.

Pecuniae imperare oportet, non servire.

Syrus, *Maxims*

Thieves who steal from private citizens spend their lives in bonds and chains; thieves who steal from public funds spend theirs in gold and purple.

Fures privatorum in nervo atque in compedibus aetatem agunt; fures publici in auro atque in purpura.

Cato, *Praeda Militibus Dividenda*, XI, 3

A bribed judge weighs the evidence poorly.

Male verum examinat omnis corruptus iudex.

Horace, *Satirae*, II, 2, 8

Money doesn't satisfy greed; it stimulates it.

Pecunia non satiat avaritiam, sed inritat.

Syrus, *Maxims*

If you make money quickly you must economize quickly, or you'll quickly go hungry.

Qui homo mature quaesivit pecuniam, nisi eam mature parsit, mature esurit.

Plautus, *Curculio*, 380-381

**To the man seeking power the poorest man
is the most useful.**

Homini potentiam quaerenti egentissumus quisque
opportunissumus.

Sallust, *Bellum Iugurthinum*, 86, 3

False becomes true when the boss decides it is.

Falsum etiam est verum quod constituit superior.

Syrus, *Maxims*

The more law, the less justice.

Summum ius summa iniuria.

Cicero, *De Officiis*, I, 33

**Many commit the same crime and face a
different fate: that man gets the cross,
this one the crown.**

Multi committunt eadem diverso crimina fato: ille
crucem sceleris pretium tulit, hic diadema.

Juvenal, *Satirae*, XIII, 105

We shed real tears if the bankruptcy is ours.

Ploratur lacrimis amissa pecunia veris.

Juvenal, *Satirae*, XIII, 134

To receive a favour is to sell your liberty.

Beneficium accipere libertatem est vendere.

Syrus, *Maxims*

**His greatest fault was his desire not to
please the best people, but to
please the most people.**

Maximum in eo vitium est, qui non melioribus vult
placere, sed pluribus.

Seneca the Younger (attributed), *Proverbs*, 36

**Everyone would have thought him fit to rule
if only he never had.**

Omnium consensus capax imperii nisi imperasset.

Tacitus, *Historiae*, I, 49

Good laws are produced by bad morals.

Leges bonae ex malis moribus procreantur.

Macrobius, *Saturnalia*, II, 13

**The people pass many laws against your kind;
always you break them by finding
a loophole. To you laws are like boiling water that
soon grows cold.**

Rogitationis plurimas propter vox populus scivit, quas
vos rogatas rumpitis; aliquam reperitis rimam. Quasi
aquam ferventem frigidum esse, ita vos putatis legis.

Plautus, *Curculio*, 508-510

No one, especially in business, can prosper if he believes what he's told.

Numquam autem recte faciet, qui cito credit, utique homo negotians.

Petronius, *Satyricon*, 43

I am a rich man as long as I don't pay my creditors.

Dives sum, si non reddo eis quibus debeo.

Plautus, *Curculio*, 377

**Sticking with what they think has never helped
political leaders.**

Numquam praestantibus in re publica gubernanda viris
laudata est in una sententia perpetua permansio.

Cicero, *Epistulae ad Familiares*, I, 9, 21

**If a man's poor and not a bad fellow, he's considered
worthless; if he is rich and a very bad fellow,
he's considered a good client.**

Si est pauper atque haud malus, nequam habetur;
sin dives malust, cliens frugi habetur.

Plautus, *Menaechmi*, 578-579

❖ ACHIEVEMENTS ❖

**He praised his own achievements, not without
cause but without end.**

Illum ipsum consulatum suum non sine causa sed
sine fine laudabat.

Seneca the Younger, *Dialectica*, X, 5

Neither friends nor foes could ever repay this fellow.

Hic est ille situs cui nemo civis neque hostis quibit pro
factis reddere opis pretium.

Ennius, *Saturae* (epitaph for Scipio Africanus)

**Uh-oh! I think I'm becoming a god.
[said by the Emperor Vespasian when dying]**

Puto dis fio.

Suetonius, *Divus Vespasianus*, XXIII, 3

**The mountain groaned loudly in great labour, then
bore a tiny mouse.**

Parturiunt montes, nascetur ridiculus mus.

Horace, *Ars Poetica*, 9

Fame comes too late to the dead.

Cineri gloria sera venit.

Martial, *Epigrammata*, XXV, 8

You can find good luck easier than you can keep it.

Fortunam citius reperias quam retineas.

Syrus, *Maxims*

Consider yourself a great orator if you can talk yourself into unpleasant duties.

Oratorem te puta, si tibi ipsi quod oportet persuaseris.

Syrus, *Maxims*

Fortune favours the brave.

Fortis fortuna adiuvat

Terence, *Phormio*, 203

LITERATURE & LEARNING

❖ ❖

No madman has ever dreamed up anything so weird that some philosopher will not say it.

Postremo nemo aegrotus quidquam somniat tam infandum, quod non aliquis dicat philosophus.

Varro, *Fragmenta*

Shallowness is natural; conceit comes with education.

Ingenita levitas et erudita vanitas.

Cicero, *Pro Flacco*

Explaining a bad saying makes it worse.

Male dictum interpretando facias acrius.

Syrus, *Maxims*

**Why are you laughing? Change the name,
and the story's yours.**

Quid rides? Mutato nomine, de te fabula narratur.

Horace, *Satirae*, I, 1, 69

**No poet or speechmaker ever
thought anybody was cleverer than he.**

Nemo umquam neque poeta neque orator fuit, qui
quemquam meliorem quam se arbitrater.

Cicero, *Epistulae ad Atticum*, XIV, 20, 3

I only spout poetry when my feet hurt.

Numquam poetor nisi podager.

Ennius, *Saturae*

**They say they memorize a lot of verses.
That's why some stay in training twenty years.**

Magnum numerum versuum (Druides) ediscere
dicuntur. Itaque annos non nulli vicenos in disciplina
permanent.

Caesar, *De Bello Gallico*, VI, 14, 4

He's either going crazy or writing verse.

Aut insanit homo aut versus facit.

Horace, *Satirae*, II, 7, 117

Water drinkers don't write good verse.

Nulla placere diu nec vivere carmina possunt quae
scribuntur aquae potoribus.

Horace, *Epistulae*, I, 19, 2

**Here are some good things, some so-so, and some bad.
There's no other way to make a book.**

Sunt bona, sunt quaedam mediocria, sunt plura mala,
quae legis hic: aliter non fit, Avite, liber.

Martial, *Epigrammata*, XV, 16

When I try to be brief, I speak gobbledegook.

Brevis esse laboro obscurus fio.

Horace, *Ars Poetica*, 25

**Neither gods, men nor booksellers tolerate
second-rate poets.**

Mediocribus esse poetis non homines, non di, non
concessere columnae.

Horace, *Ars Poetica*, 372

If it's well said, I said it.

Quicquid bene dictum est ab ullo meum est.

Seneca the Younger, *Epistulae Morales*, XVI, 7

**Book, if you're lucky you'll be loved in Rome;
if you're unlucky, you'll be chewed by bookworms
and forgotten; if you're very unlucky,
you might become a textbook.**

Liber, caris eris Romae, donec te deserat aetas;
aut tineas pasces taciturnus inertes, aut pueros
elementa docens manes.

Horace, *Epistulae*, I, 20 (paraphrased)

**Charming girls are won by poetry,
greedy ones by presents; you'll show your nature
when you get these verses.**

Carmine formosae, pretio capiuntur avarae; gaudeat, ut
digna est, versibus illa novis.

Lygdamus, *Corpus Tibullianum* (addendum)

**When the learned men appeared,
the good ones went missing.**

Postquam docti prodierunt, boni desunt.

Seneca the Younger, *Epistulae Morales*, XCV, 13

**The book you're reading is mine, Fidentinus;
but your lousy rendition is making it yours.**

Quem recitas meus est, o Fidentine, libellus: sed male
cum recitas, incipit esse tuus.

Martial, *Epigrammata*, I, 38

**Why don't I send you my poems to read, Pontilianus?
I'm afraid that you might send me yours.**

Cur non mitte meos tibi, Pontiliane, libellos?
Ne mihi tu mittas, Pontiliane, tuos.

Martial, *Epigrammata*, VII, 3

Anybody with a brain flees a versifying poet.

Vesanum poetam qui sapiunt fugiunt.

Horace, *Ars Poetica*, 455

Paulus buys poems and recites them as his own. What you paid good money for you can call yours.

Carmina Paulus emit. Recitat sua carmina Paulus. Nam quod emas, possis iure vocare tuum.

Martial, *Epigrammata*, II, 20

**You publish no poems, yet you carp at mine.
Publish your work or shut up.**

Cum tua non edas, carpis mea carmina, Laeli.
Carpere vel noli nostra vel ede tua.

Martial, *Epigrammata*, I, 91

**Plague take those who said our wise words
before we did.**

Pereant qui ante nos nostra dixerunt.

St Jerome, *In Ecclestiasten Commentarius*, I

**You don't recite, and you want to be thought a poet.
Be whatever you like; just don't recite.**

Nil recitas et vis, Mamerce, poeta videri.
Quidquid vis esto, dummodo nil recites.

Martial, *Epigrammata*, II, 88

**If only dead poets are praised,
I'd rather go unsung.**

Nec laudas nisi mortuos poetas: tanti non est,
ut placeam, perire.

Martial, *Epigrammata*, VIII, 49

To write without clarity and charm is a miserable waste of time and ink.

Mandare quemquam litteris cogitationes suas, qui eas nec disponere nec illustrare possit nec delectatione aliqua adlicere lectorem, hominis est intemperanter abutentis et otio et litteris.

Cicero, *Tusculanae Disputationes*, I, 2, 4

They praise good books, they read the bad ones.

Laudant illa sed ista legunt.

Martial, *Epigrammata*, IV, 49

❖ RELATIONSHIPS ❖

I felt more sorrow in his going than joy in his coming.

Plus aegri ex abitu viri, quam ex adventu voluptatis cepi.

Plautus, *Amphitruo*, 634

You may try many times before finding a good man.

Multa ante temptes quam virum invenias bonum.

Syrus, *Maxims*

**When you view your own sins your eyes are dim
and sickly; so why, for a friend's failings, do you
have the sight of an eagle?**

Cum tua pervideas oculis mala lippus inunctis; cur in
amicorum vitiis tam cernis acutum quam aquila?

Horace, *Satirae*, III, 25-27

**Postumus, once you were sane; are you really
taking a wife?**

Certe sanus eras; uxore, Postume, ducis?

Juvenal, *Satirae*, VI, 28

**On the tombs of seven husbands she inscribed:
'Chloe made this'.
What could be more honest?**

Inscripsit tumulis septem scelerata virorum:
'Se fecisse Chloe'.
Quid pote simplicius?

Martial, *Epigrammata*, IX, 15

**If you expect your friend to be unoffended by your
warts, you'd better pardon his pimples.**

Qui ne tuberibus propriis offendat amicum postulat,
ignoscet verrucis illius.

Horace, *Satirae*, I, 3, 74-75

**Why does that door scare you?
Because my beastly wife is right behind it.**

Quid has metuis fores?
Conclusam hic habeo uxorem saevam.

Terence, *Phormio*, 744

**All the friends she had Lycoris has buried. I keep
hoping she'll befriend my wife.**

Omnes quas habuit, Fabiane, Lycoris amicas extulit.
Uxori fiat amica meae.

Martial, *Epigrammata*, IV, 24

**To have a good wife is charming, if there is any place
one can be found.**

Bona uxor suave ductust, si sit usquam gentium ubi ea
possit inveniri.

Plautus, *Miles Gloriosus*, 686

**Just like your furniture, Paulus, your friends
are antiques.**

Si tamquam tabulas scyphosque, Paule, omnes
archetypos habes amicos.

Martial, *Epigrammata*, XII, 69

What a pleasant stain comes from an enemy's blood.

Iucunda macula est ex inimici sanguine.

Syrus, *Maxims*

Seeing that you are very well-matched, he the worst possible husband, you the worst possible wife, I wonder why you are not well content.

Cum sitis similes paresque vita, uxor pessima,
pessimus maritus, miror non bene
convenire vobis.

Martial, *Epigrammata*, VIII, 35

Censor: 'So help you Heaven, have you a wife?'
Witness: 'I have a wife, Heaven help me.'

Censor: 'Ex tui animi sententia tu uxorem habes?'
Index: 'Non hercle, ex mei animi sententia.'

Cicero (quoted in *De Oratore*, II)

You've just buried your seventh rich wife
in that field. Nobody gets more
out of a farm than you do.

Septima iam, Phileros, tibi conditur uxor in agro.
Plus nulli, Phileros, quam tibi reddit ager.

Martial, *Epigrammata*, X, 43

The word friend is common, the fact is rare.

Vulgare amici nomen, sed rara est fides.

Phaedrus, *Fabulae*, III, 9, 1

My wife torments me. Why? She won't die.

Uxor me excruciat. Cur? Quia vivit.

Plautus, *Casina*, 227

**When Fortune leaves you,
so do your friends.**

Stat nulla diu mortalibus usquam,
Fortuna titubante, fides.

Silius Italicus, *Punica*, XI, 3

**Always dread your lady's birthday:
dark is the day that demands a present.**

Magna superstitio tibi sit natalis amicae: quaque aliquid
dandum est, illa sit atra dies.

Ovid, *Ars Amatoria*, I, 417-418

❖ LOVE ❖

In love, beauty counts for more than good advice.

In amore forma plus valet quam auctoritas.

Syrus, *Maxims*

If you want to be loved, be lovable!

Ut ameris, amabilis esto!

Ovid, *Ars Amatoria*, II, 107

**Without food and drink,
love will grow cold.**

Sine Cerere et Libero friget Venus.

Terence, *Eunuchus*, 732

**You say all the lovely girls burn for love of you,
Sextus, but your face looks always looks like
you're swimming under water.**

Dicis amore tui bellas ardere puellas, qui faciem
sub aqua, Sexte, natantis, habes.

Martial, *Epigrammata*, II, 87

A lover, like a torch, burns brighter when shaken.

Amans, sicut fax, agitando ardescit magis.

Syrus, *Maxims*

Take care that you never declare war on Cupid.

Cave sis cum Amore tu unquam bellum sumpseris.

Plautus, *Cistellaria*, 300

I believe love first devised the torturer's profession for mankind.

Credo ego Amorem primum apud homines carnificinam commentum.

Plautus, *Cistellaria*, 203

A woman loves you or she hates you; there's no other choice.

Aut amat aut odit mulier; nihil est tertium.

Syrus, *Maxims*

**Show me a lover with self-control,
and I'll give you his weight in gold.**

Auro contra cedo modestum amatorem,
a me aurum accipe.

Plautus, *Curculio*, 201

**What a woman says to a panting lover
should be written on the wind and
running water.**

Mulier cupido quod dicit amanti, in vento
et rapida scribere oportet aqua.

Catullus, *Veronensis Liber*, 70

You're a new kind of lover if you're ashamed of anything you do.

Novo modo tu homo amas, siquidem te quicquam quod faxis pudet.

Plautus, *Miles Gloriosus*, 624

No one is able to flee from death or love.

Nec mortem effugere quisquam nec amorem potest.

Syrus, *Maxims*

Every love dies when a new one comes along.

Successore novo vincitur omnis amor.

Ovid, *Remedia Amoris*, 343

**I shall not ape other comic lovers,
who sigh to the night or day or sun or moon;
none of whom give a fig for man's concerns.**

Non ego item facio ut alios in comoediis vi vidi
amoris facere, qui aut nocti aut die aut soli aut lunae
miserias narrant suas; quos pol ego credo humanas
querimonias non tanti facere.

Plautus, *Mercator*, 4-5

An absent love vanishes and a new one takes its place.

Vanescitque absens et novus intrat amor.

Ovid, *Ars Amatoria*, II, 358

A fellow who sets out on love's road with an empty
purse is taking on greater labours than Hercules.

Qui amans egens ingressus est princeps in Amoris vias,
superavit aerumnis suis aerumnas Herculi.

Plautus, *Persa*, 1-2

Who can really deceive a lover?

Quis fallere possit amantem?

Virgil, *Aeneid*, IV, 296

I don't think anyone knows I love the girl;
I haven't done anything really silly yet.

Non vereor ne illam me amare hic potuerit resciscere;
quippe haud etiam quicquam inepte feci.

Plautus, *Mercator*, 380-381

**The gods never let us love and be wise
at the same time.**

Amare et sapere vix deo conceditur.

Syrus, *Maxims*

The perjured oaths of lovers carry no penalty.

Amantis ius iurandum poenam non habet.

Syrus, *Maxims*

❖ WOMEN ❖

**Some tragic poet said two women are
worse than one. That's true.**

Antiquom poetam audivi scripsisse in tragoedia
mulieres duas peiores esse quam una; res itast.

Plautus, *Curculio*, 591

**Beautiful clothes win us; jewels and gold cover
everything; very little of our love is for the girl herself.**

Auferimur cultu; gemmis auroque teguntur omnia; par
minima est ipsa puella sui.

Ovid, *Remedia Amoris*, 343-344

A woman's always better seen than heard.

Tacitast melior mulier semper quam loquens.

Plautus, *Rudens*, 1114

**Thais' teeth are black, Laecania's are white.
What is the difference? Thais has her own.**

Thais habet nigros, niveos Laecania dentes.
Quae ratio est? Emptos haec habet, illa suos.

Martial, *Epigrammata*, V, 43

**A dowry is a wonderful source of money.
Only if it comes without the wife.**

Pulchra edepol dos pecuniast. Quae quidem pol
non maritast.

Plautus, *Epidicus*, 180

**Long before Helen's day a wench was the
worst cause of war.**

Nam fuit ante Helenam cunnus taeterrima belli causa

Horace, *Satirae*, I, 3, 107

**Sounds like you're saying there's no such thing
as a good woman.
Not at all; I never state an obvious fact.**

Quasi dicas nullam mulierem bonam esse.
Haud equidem dico, nec mos meust ut praedicem quod
ego omnes scire credam.

Plautus, *Mercator*, 512-513

Women outshine men in scheming.

Malo in consilio feminae vincunt viros.

Syrus, *Maxims*

**She's the one woman worthy to compare to you, sir.
By Hercules, what a beauty she must be!**

Ad tuam formam illa una dignast.
Hercle pulchram praedicas.

Plautus, *Miles Gloriosus*, 968

I really liked her once she died.

Placere occepit graviter, postquam emortuast.

Caecilius Statius, *Plocium*

A woman smells best when she doesn't smell at all.

Ecastor mulier recte olet, ubi nihil olet.

Plautus, *Mostellaria*, 273

When a woman is openly bad she at last is good.

Aperte mala cum est mulier, tum demum est bona.

Syrus, *Maxims*

Women learn to tell lies by weeping.

Didicere flere feminae in mendacium.

Syrus, *Maxims*

Now's the time for bad girls to become worse still.

Edepol nunc nos tempus est malas peioris fieri.

Plautus, *Miles Gloriosus*, 1218

Woman is surely the daughter of Delay.

Mulier profecto natast ex ipsa Mora.

Plautus, *Miles Gloriosus*, 1292

No woman was lovelier than you, Lycoris;
no woman is lovelier than Glycera.
She will be what you are; you cannot be what she is.
How times change! I want her; I wanted you.

Femina praeferri potuit tibi nulla, Lycori;
praeferri Glycerae femina nulla potest.
Haec erit hoc quod tu; tu non potes esse quod haec est.
Tempora quid faciunt! Hanc volo; te volui.

Martial, *Epigrammata*, VI, 40

Woman is always a slippery, changeable thing.

Varium et mutabile semper femina.

Virgil, *Aeneid*, IV, 569

No cavalry or infantry has the gall to manoeuvre as coolly as a woman can.

Neque eques neque pedes profectost quisquam tanta audacia, si aeque faciat confidenter quicquam quam mulier facit.

Plautus, *Miles Gloriosus*, 466-467

When a woman speaks sweetly, she's plotting mischief.

Dulce de labris loquuntur, corde vivunt noxio.

Florus, *De Qualitate Vitae*, III

**Paula, you want to marry Priscus; you're wise.
Priscus doesn't want to marry you; he's also wise.**

Nubere vis Prisco: non miror, Paula; sapisti.
Ducere te non vult Priscus; et ille sapit.

Martial, *Epigrammata*, IX, 5

If she has as many years as hairs on her head, she's three.

Toto vertice quot gerit capillos annos si tot habet Ligeia trima est.

Martial, *Epigrammata*, XII, 7

Trust your ship to the winds, not your heart to the girls; waves are safer than women.

Crede ratem ventis, animum ne crede puellis; namque est feminea tutior unda fide.

Pentadius, *De Femina*

When women equal men, they'll run the show.

Simul ac (mulieres) pares esse coeperint, superiores
erunt.

Cato (quoted by Livy)

You send me a hare to eat and always say:
'You'll be beautiful in seven days.'
If you haven't been lying to me, my sweet, you clearly
never ate a hare yourself.

Si quando leporem mittis mihi, Gellia, dicis:
'Formosus septem, Marce, diebus eris.'
Si non derides, si verum, lux mea, narras, edisti
numquam, Gellia, tu leporem.

Martial, *Epigrammata*, V, 29

❖ AMUSEMENTS ❖

THE THEATRE

If sickness kept you from the play, you have better luck than sense.

Si infirmatas valetudinis tuae tenuit quominus ad ludos venires, fortunae magis tribuo quam sapientiae.

Cicero, *Ad Familiares*, VII, 1

If you were well and chose not to come, I'm glad both your body and judgement are in good shape.

Si per valitudinem posses venire tamen noluisti, te sine dolore corporis fuisse et animo valuisse laetor.

Cicero, *Ad Familiares*, VII, 1

Some come to see; some come to be seen.

Spectatum veniunt; veniunt spectentur.

Ovid, *Ars Amatoria*, I, 99

**First on the stage for the sake of their honour were those
who should have left it for the sake of their honour.**

Primum honoris causa in scaenam redierant ii, quos ego
honoris causa de scaena decesse arbitrabar.

Cicero, *Ad Familiares*, VII, 1

**If during the play you read anything except my orations,
you had more fun than we had.**

Si quidvis potius quam orationes meas legeris, plus quam
quisquam nostrum delectationis habuisti.

Cicero, *Ad Familiares*, VII, 1

THE RACES

**They don't care for fast horses or good drivers now,
just the colours they wear.
That's too much power in one cheap tunic.**

Neque velocitate equorum neque hominum arte
traherentur, favent colore.
Tanta gratia, tanta auctoritas in una vilissima tunica.

Pliny the Younger, *Epistulae*, IX, 6

❖ MISCELLANEA ❖

The gods use us mortals as footballs.

Di nos quasi pilas homines habent.

Plautus, *Captivi, Prologus*, 22

**Diaulus used to be a doctor, now he's an undertaker.
His clients still end up in the same state.**

Nuper erat medicus, nunc est vespillo Diaulus.
Quod vespillo facit, fecerat et medicus.

Martial, *Epigrammata*, I, 47

Volusens returned to Caesar, having seen all [of Britain] a man could who didn't dare get out of his ship.

Volusenus, perspectis regionibus quantum ei facultatis dari potuit qui ex navi egredi ad Caesarem revertitur.

Caesar, *De Bello Gallico*, IV, 21, 31

You wonder why travel did not improve you? You had yourself for a travelling companion.

Quaeris quare te fuga ista non adiuvet? Tecum fugis.

Seneca the Younger, *Epistulae Morales*, XXXVIII, 11

**This wine is forty years old.
It certainly doesn't show its age.**

Hoc vinum Falernum annorum quadragenta est.
Bene aetatem fert.

Cicero (quoted in Macrobius' *Saturnalia*, II, 3)

**In your fine new clothes you mock my scruffy toga.
It may be scruffy, Zoilus, but it's paid for.**

Penatus pulchre rides mea, Zoile, trita. Sunt haec trita
quidem, Zoile, sed mea sunt.

Martial, *Epigrammata*, II, 58

The monkey is repulsive; he's much too much like us!

Simia quam similes turpissima bestia nobis!

Ennius, *Saturae*

**The wrath of the gods may be great,
but it certainly is slow.**

Ut sit magna, tamen certe lenta ira deorum est.

Juvenal, *Satirae*, XIII, 100

**Come with deathless poems and all the Muses; if you
bring no gift, Homer, out you go.**

Ipse licet venias Musis comitatus, Homere; si nihil
attuleris, ibis, Horace, foras.

Ovid, *Ars Amatoria*, II, 280

Some, through fear of death, prayed to die.

Quidam timore mortis mortem orabant.

Pliny the Younger, *Epistula Cornelio Tacito*

The bravest Gauls are the Belgians, because they are far away from the blessings of civilization.

Horum omnium fortissimi sunt Belgae, propterea quod a cultu atque humanitate provinciae absunt.

Caesar, *De Bello Gallico*, I, 1, 6

What shall I say about the usefulness of spreading manure?

Quid de utilitate loquar stercorandi?

Cicero, *De Senectute*, XV, 54
(Cicero was an amateur farmer and an excellent politician)

**For Heaven's sake, why are you and cheerfulness
complete strangers?**

Quid, cedo, te obsecro tam abhorret hilaritudo?

Plautus, *Cistellaria*, 54

Don't wish ill for your enemy; plan it.

De inimico non loquaris sed cogites.

Syrus, *Maxims*

**Why do I enjoy my farm so much, Linus?
I never see you there.**

Quid mihi reddat ager quaeris, Line Nomentanus?
Hoc mihi reddat ager: te, Line, non video.

Martial, *Epigrammata*, II, 38

Beware of Greeks bearing gifts.

Timeo Danaos et dona ferentes.

Virgil, *Aeneid*, II, 49

If I can't move Heaven, I'll raise Hell.

Flectere si nequeo superos, Acheronta movebo.

Virgil, *Aeneid*, VII, 312

I am what you will be.

Quod sum eris.

Epitaph on Roman tombstone

AUTHORS

St Augustine, Aurelius Augustinus AD 354 – 430
St Jerome, Eusebius Hieronymus AD c. 340 – 420
Caecilius, Statius c: 219 – 166 BC
Caesar, Gaius Julius 100 – 44 BC
Cato, Marcus Porcius 234 – 149 BC
Catullus, Gaius Valerius c. 84 – c. 54 BC
Cicero, Marcus Tullius 106 – 43 BC
Ennius, Quintus 239 – 169 BC
Florus, Publius Annius c. AD 74
Gellius, Aulus c. AD 123 – 165
Horatius Flaccus, Quintus 65 – 8 BC
Juvenalis, Decimus Iunius c. AD 60 – 117
Livius Andronicus, Lucius c. 280 – c. 204 BC
Lygdamus c. 43 BC – c. AD 1
Macrobius, Ambrosius Theodosius c. AD 400
Martialis, Marcus Valerius c. AD 40 – c. 104
Nepos, Cornelius c. 100 – c. 25 BC
Ovidius Naso, Publius 43 BC – AD 17
Pentadius c. AD 290
Persius Flaccus, Aulus AD 34 – 62
Petronius Arbiter, Gaius c. AD 26 – 66
Phaedrus, Gaius Iulius c. 15 BC – c. AD 45
Plautus, Titus Maccius c. 255 – 184 BC
Plinius Caecilius Secundus, Gaius c. AD 61 – 114
Prudentius, Aurelius Clemens AD 348 – c. 405
Quintilianus, Marcus Fabius c. AD 35 – c. 95
Sallustius Crispus, Gaius c. 86 – c. 35 BC
Seneca, Lucius Annaeus (the Elder) c. 55 BC – AD 37
Seneca, Lucius Annaeus (the Younger) c. 4 BC – AD 65
Silius Italicus, Tiberius Catius Asconius AD 26 – 101
Suetonius, Tranquillus Gaius AD 70 – 140
Syrus, Publilius c. 85 – 43 BC
Tacitus, Publius Cornelius c. AD 55 – 117
Terentius Afer, Publius c. 185 – 159 BC
Varro, Marcus Terentius 116 – 27 BC
Vergilius Maro, Publius 70 – 19 BC